# SCARECROW ORACLE

*poems*

## Mark L. Anderson

KORREKTIV PRESS

[seattle • new orleans •
copenhagen]

For permissions and ordering information, visit
www.korrektivpress.com

10 9 8 7 6 5 4 3 2 1

Cover art by Tiffany Patterson
Layout and design by Thom Caraway
Author photo by Dean Davis

ISBN: 978-0-9831513-6-4
LCCN: 2022935277

# CONTENTS

Part 3

# GOING BACKWARD TO WHERE IT STARTS

I write this poem. I have a scar on my cheek that looks like a dimple. I am scared. A woman screams at her boyfriend not to jump from the bridge. The Earth revolves around the sun. I close my eyes and open them. A chow-dog named Yogi becomes dead. I lie. My parents ask if I know why Yogi bit me. Yogi tears my cheek open with his teeth. I yank Yogi by the collar under the unflinching summer sun. I like dogs. I make up prayers and believe them. I am born. My parents have sex. My parents meet at a diner on Sunset Highway. My mother is a waitress. My father is a construction worker. Life is not as easy as my parents had hoped it would be. My parents need love. My parents are born. Life is lonely for everyone and no one knows why. The Earth revolves around the sun. People kill each other over what they think happens after death. Humanity exists. Life exists on a small, rocky planet. Space debris collides around a young star forming a small, rocky planet. Our star is birthed in explosion in an outer arm of the Milky Way. Briefly, the universe is the same size as you are, right now, reading this poem. Bang.

# ONE

# GROWING UP THISTLES

Boys tear asphalt
from a country road,

hurl the chunks like laughter,
not really wanting to hurt

each other, but not surprised
either when red flowers through

the creviced skin like a thistle's
crown rising

from the tiny cracks in the road.
You'd call it impossible if

you didn't know better, for such
a tiny crack to let in enough light

for life to search for more. You'd call
it ugly if you couldn't see

that sharp shadow
silhouetted against black-top,

haloed by the burning sky's stare,
swaying in the wind like a dance

with the bony shadows of two boys:
one, the skeleton of a great bird,

letting go of innocence
like a rock, the other

sinking inward,
touching his ear as a shimmer

drips to the ground.

# THE ELVES AND THE SHOEMAKER AT MICA CEMETERY

It is difficult to make a living
as a shoemaker in the Mica Cemetery.

No one has been buried there
for forty years. But everyone knows
elves make the best cobblers

and there are plenty of those. Plenty
to service these little, red bricks

almost covered by wild grasses:
no letters on them. A mother
walking with her son frowns

before the markers as the boy
asks what they are. The elves

below are single-celled organisms
called paramecium or "tiny slippers,"
hammering away at first pairs

of shoes for lost children.
*Times were hard*, the mother explains.

*Children died so often. Parents
couldn't afford headstones.* The spring sun
will be setting soon, burying

the yellow sky behind wiry branches,
a fairy circle almost ready

to blossom. *It must have hurt
so much.* They walk homeward as elves
continue the tired shoemaker's job.

He will arrive in the morning, amazed.
His job is nearly done. Soon, even the nameless

will walk out from this place in peace.

# INNOCENCE

Innocence left us like a firefly
escaping a glass jar. It went
to live in a coastal hamlet
with pastel crayon roofs
that slope yellow and blue,
where perhaps people are not
cruel as children's laughter.
*Fine*, we said when it left,
but even with all the electric
light bulbs in the world
we have trouble seeing
the good in each other.
I imagine Innocence took work
as a confectioner. It rises early
to bake lush strawberry fields
into gumdrop cakes.
When adults complain its flavors
lack complexity, it does not resort
to bitterness. Every night
it screams into the ocean.
It wants us to believe in the importance
of the seagull diving beneath
the wave, in the small, magical
life in the sand. But instead,
we clench our hearts, knowing
any moment our scars could come
unzipped. What then? The world's
gone mad. I hate to say it,
but I fear it's nothing new.

We write letters to Innocence
and cork them in bottles,
hoping the tide delivers
to the correct address.
We promise a homecoming
parade: floats and marching bands,
balloons that soar so high
they never have to come back down.
We promise this time we'll do better.
When a butterfly settles into our palm
we will not pin it to the wall.

# CHILDREN DISCOVER AN ELECTRIC FENCE AND THE DIRECTION OF TIME

The wire tongue of lightning
                hisses *listen* to the children

growing up before it
                in the brown-green muck

gazing in on the horses
                and their held-in stampede

the electric voice speaks
                *lift this knowledge from my palm*

*like fruit, the language you're made of*
                *the music the universe sings*

*enclosing yearning in the muscles*
                *of these mud-covered mahogany*

*beasts galloping small*
                *arcs back and forth*

the children hesitant step
                closer to the hypnotic buzz

entering into its note
                ignoring the mother

her face a snapshot of shock
                        an expression ancient as the days

as the people who measured them
                        who painted horses like magic

onto rock walls rising out of rivers
                        where stones roll in the currents

eroding into tiny grains
                        of silt in an hourglass

turned over into the widening oceans
                        of the children's eyes swelling

with the spirit of the first wild horse
                        of the first to believe they could be ridden.

# ON THE FIRST DAY OF SPRING

Many as the leaves of a willow
weeping over the slow river
are the ounces of starlight
many as the leaves in the fall
for a moment flying a moment
waving goodbye saying I made it
my own way like I said to you shivering
my hand life is not a failure
because it ends all these little lives
bloom because they must
*I saw delight shatter worlds* blue
hand in a vial of starlight
shivered by the fabric of a dress
blue as an orchid can be blue
floating in the night on a slow river
a small dying in every breath
many as the valleys of my hand
every triumphant goodbye drinking
sorrows plentiful as the stars
in the black orchid sky every sorrow
blooming like the morning, like a cease-fire,
like a song—
        it will be something beautiful.

# SO YOU WANT ME TO FALL IN LOVE WITH YOU

My first nightmare felt so real I was
terrified for years. It's funny now.
I never met a ten-foot-tall hairy demon
with ox horns anywhere else.
I can still see it though. Don't eat
me please oh monster. So you want me

to fall in love with you and you're wondering
if I'm still a child, or maybe you're the silly one and
I'm the stuffed animal, but one of us is definitely
afraid of the dark. That's the problem
with stuffed animals. Everyone gets bigger
around them and they still feel so small.

I wanted my mom to link arms with me
so that when the monster came and I died
my soul wouldn't float away.
She didn't know what was wrong with this
child who had never seen death but felt it
all around him. *There's no monsters honey*
*let me tell you a story, hug this stuffed*
*platypus your sister bought you with her*
*own money. You're not going to die. One*
*day you'll be all grown up and you'll*
*leave me but that's okay.* And I said I might
leave but I'll come back. And I'll always
have a room in my house for you. She smiled
and I'm sure cried with a complex grown-up
emotion once I had finally fallen to sleep.
*One day, little one, you'll have children of your own*
*and they'll be all grown up*
*and they'll leave you too.*

22

I was eleven years old and Joe was dying, and I
barely even knew him, but two days before
he passed I held his hand and said all the
right things that nobody else could say.
My mom and my aunt were speechless
when I told him he'd done enough,
and it wasn't any use being sorry or afraid
for anything anymore, and that there is love
after death. I still thought kissing
or church bells were where babies came from.
He'd been waiting all his life to be told those things.

I still wake at night thinking about death.
That's the problem with stuffed animals.
They are good at comforting everyone else
but cannot feel their own hearts beat.

I take a hatchet to my walls.

I light a signal fire and hope it gets to someone.

I hope one of you can tell me what this means.

## HIDE-A-BED STORY

The bed, folded back into a couch, grumbles
like a troubled stomach as my mother, not yet panicking,
wonders, *now where did my little boy go?*

# DANDELIONS

Dandelions are the best flower
because they are the only flower
made of wishes.

Maybe you are a wish.
Love is a good wish,
a child's secret carried off by the wind.

The child picks these tiny, yellow deaths,
snaps their stems between his index finger and thumb
arranging a bouquet for his mother

who smiles at so many of them
gathered at once,
seeing wishes she made when she was his size,

before she understood what it meant
that she will grow old and die,
then he will grow old and die,

then even his children will grow old and die.
And that is how their lives will unfold
if we are so lucky.

But hey,
wishes turn into dandelions when they die.
Did you know that?

They reach up like suns
grasping at the sky that is their birthright.
Then the child transforms them into a symbol

for love. Look, magic—
one thing turns into another
and we don't know how or why.

Like his hands,
at first they can only grasp and release.
They can only open and close

transforming everything they touch.
They can only give and take
holding up a shoe-box

containing the deceased body
of the world's best hamster,
the fountain of youth amassing on his cheeks,

dripping to the ground
where dandelions turn from yellow to white
in a single night's whisper.

But this isn't about dandelions anymore, is it?
In this moment the child learns
how the imperfect mechanism of his hand

cannot hold onto everything he loves.
He can't even hold onto that hamster.
He can't catch it when it escapes his grasp.

But he sits down and hears a skull crack beneath the chair,
an ugly precursor to music
too small for the significance it carries,

like his hands offering up a shoe-box
made heavy by the question of death,
pleading for his mother to fix it.

When she inevitably can't
he looks up to her and says,
*There is no mommy magic, is there?*

The child gets bigger every time she looks at him.
He turns into me.
Look, magic—

one thing turns into another
and we have to believe it's a good thing.
I pick an old dandelion turned wise with age,

whisper into its ear a question regarding loss.
In response, it lets go of everything it has ever been.

# ON THE SIZE OF WINGS

Pegasus, you silly horse-moth,
we draw your wingspan to please
our eyes.  You'd need wings

the size of skyscrapers to carry
your heavy, galloping hooves,
to race across the white tops

of wind-blown clouds, where
I'm sure you are as disappointed
as I am to not find heaven.

Instead, we depict slim avian
appendages on your back, as if
they could carry anyone. It should

be beautiful bells up there, not
just thinner air. We draw you
not as you need, but as we like.

Like heaven, an uncertainty
too large and unwieldy to make
into art. Silly hawk-ellope.

Forgive us for not being reasonable.
We put together our favorite
kinds of freedom to create you.

# FOREGROUND, BACKGROUND

Summer grass bends green under my feet as Dad
throws the baseball, *Catch!* And I might be there,
even now, twenty years in the foreground. The baseball,

a cloud of stained leather, its stitches a blur against
the sky going yellow with day, pauses mid-air. In the
background is a crawl space that has yet to take up residence

in my dreams. Here, the crawl space is where I take
action figures, pose great battles, before the muck and earwigs
and mysteries burrow like terror into my bloodstream.

I think of when living is over, and I see this place. I picture
being trapped there without even a flashlight, only this time
it doesn't end, and I push up against it with my legs,

but it doesn't budge, like that time my brother barricaded
the entrance, stuffed in a hose and let flow cold water,
and I kicked against the underside of the deck until

our mom heard, and my tongue tasted like metal, and that place,
like dreams, was held together by rusting nails with crags
sticking out, and your shirt catches on them and rips,

and when you wake from this dream unable to move
you want your mother to take you in her arms, burn peroxide
over your wounds, shaking her head. *You kids ruin all*

*your new clothes.* Just what is she going to do with me,
looking out the grimed kitchen window at the empty lot
with the grass so tall a kid could get lost in it, *what if we*

*put up a fence?* I might be there, even now, as she opens
an envelope, makes a joke about bills I don't yet understand.
What if I come out of that crawl space covered in worms,

and death is not a dream, but my mitt is open, greased,
I'm breaking it in as the dragonflies make long circles
overhead. My father is still young and my legs itch just

above the sock, so thin they might be blades of grass
pushing up from where the dead kick with their iron boots,
right there where the crickets chirp down the end of summer.

# TWO

# WHAT COMES DOWN

The barn door is open, the feet stomp and jump,
shake the whole town, shake the town down,
one night a week to get it all out. Are you going
down, down, down, we ask of each other. Down
to the river, down to the barn, down to the ground.
We are going. We can't stop going. We drink
and we dance because we cannot stop from going.
Good-bye, good-bye, we wave from the ground.

The music wails once a week. We make the love
we must and then we sleep. And when we sleep we dream,
great dreams out of this small town. Out of the dirt, the mud
and the grain. But we are children of the grain.

It's lies, it's all lies. I come from this place but I am not
from it. I sing the song of this place, but I am not
singing it. I grew up in a small town seventy years removed
from the barn. But I did grow up with a barn.

It was a church once, actually. Once a week people stomped
into the doors to speak with their Lord. And their prayers
went up. And when I lived there swallows and bats
came down through the bell tower. And we shot bees

and their nests down with bb guns. That was my
American anthem. Brutality, beasts, bugs, and a group
of boys living in the shell of prayers long gone.
But the place stomped. Every night I would hear a stomp,
stomp, and I'd say *It's the wind, wind.* The truth is
I've worried that the stories I inhabit are not fully American.

I lay in my bed with the television infomercials breaking
down sense, chasing away the spirits, the white, lazy
ceiling flickering blue then dark, and I thought of the prayers
generations offered up, of the people who died,
who are not remembered by history. It's impossible
to track their stories down. They're indistinguishable from lies.

My mother stomps in through the doorway, static on her face,
saying my uncle has died. And that doorway has been torn down.
I would change death if I could. I would let us hold
onto each other forever. No childhood home would be destroyed.
My uncle lay under a thin, white sheet, an arm poking out
I could see the life had departed from. My Aunt said *I hate this,*
*God. Bring him back.* I inhabit the exoskeleton of these memories.
I speak of them as if I truly remember. People
paced in circles, a frenetic swarm of bees who'd lost
their hive. At band class the next day my tears blurred
the sheet music until I could no longer play.
*My uncle died last night,* I said, not believing myself.

And the story goes on, impossible to beat into a myth.
Bees nest inside my rusted-through Chevy. I think
I'm not an American story without leaving those I love. People
curse a God who takes away lives indiscriminately as a child
with a gun. I didn't cry for four years. We go down.
We lose what we have. Hope stomps back up from the ground.

The door is open. The music wails on. The mouth tells the story
again, each time with different words: each time the same.

# SAINT OF SPOKANE VALLEY

Car-lots and cars, showgirls and mechanics,
six-lane roads, burnt-out bars, sickly tall pines;
redeem this place says the cloud-grey fall.
Redeem the squalor, the forest, the aluminum
can blowing across a six-lane road,
or let it go: let it all go for good.

I remember my uncle was basically good,
crawling under cars, a proud mechanic.
If your car broke down he'd get it back on the road
and driving through this sickly city of pines.
Back on the farm, only cans were aluminum,
and the leaves only went grey in the fall.

Saint of Spokane Valley, my uncle died this fall.
At his wake, his friends tell us how good
he was. They drink from aluminum
cans with cozies on them. My cousin, a mechanic,
says our uncle was his inspiration. In the pine
forest, camping, he'd get you out of the road,

off the run. Hell, we've all made mistakes. The road
to hell has six lanes. That road to the fall,
we call it Sprague. You'll never see our pain.
Death itself is basically good.
Death is a proud mechanic.
Death built us a cage of aluminum

and called it a car, said aluminum

runs forever, and we drive down that road.
Hell, it's cheap here. At least when we fail
and the car breaks down my uncle is a mechanic—
he will shoulder all of our pain.
At the funeral we call him good,

we enumerate the ways he was like Jesus. Good enough,
we find some of it true. On the floor was melted aluminum
or could that be my cousin's tears? Pain
we didn't know he had until we traveled that road.
Spokane Valley has lost its saint to the long, grey fall.
The world has lost a good mechanic.

Pain found my uncle in the road,
with aluminum hands dragged him away this fall.
God has taken away our mechanic.

# IN THE AFTERWORLD I ENCOUNTER ALL THE THINGS I'VE LOST

Vultures lift into rotten egg wind in this desert
of the afterlife, guarding my still spit-moist

retainer. Straight teeth don't matter here, but it's
on top of Platypus, my stuffed best friend. I miss him,

his fur all matted like Bud, the mud-colored mutt
we rescued half-dead, two-thirds blind, mewling

with her paws trailing red in the snow. Abandoned,
ugly Bud. Bud who just disappeared. She's here, barking

at a blue cooler, wagging up dust. The dust is really
paint chips I peeled from our front porch last summer,

turning the deck ugly, exposing it to rot. It's fun
to peel the paint off like a scab. I'd do the whole thing.

Stop barking, Bud, I'll open the lid. It must be
so dark inside that cooler where we put

our captive grasshoppers. I forgot. Went inside.
those vultures are really robins, I can see them now.

They're the baby robins that hatched by my treehouse,
that I climbed up to and pet. Their bald heads are really

cracked blue eggs. I knew their mother
might leave them to die if I reached my hand,

but I still did, giving them small,
soft strokes. What could it hurt?

Bud, I remember I wretched,  opening the lid
of that cooler—bugs baked in the heat.

It must have been so dark as the grasshoppers
writhed over each other, kicking to leap

against the plastic walls and lid with a click, click,
click that must have been the biggest thing they ever knew.

# I SPENT MY SUMMER NIGHTS ON THE PATIO OF OLD EMPYREAN

because we were young

because to be young is to be stupid

because we do not get a million nights

because age sticks its fingers into the spine

because our story didn't take long to tell

because the years ahead were quicksand
already sucking at our feet

because the train endlessly leaving town
is the spirit of every twenty-something-
year-old in this city of bricked up dreams

because when are we going to be famous?

because love is hard like the falling apart
concrete walls of an ancient train trestle

because we fancied ourselves the kings of the place

because we wanted to save rock and roll
we wanted to save poetry

because everyone laughed at us

because some of the people in this story
have already died

because innocence is a lightning bug
fading away in the smog heavy sky

because we were not original, yet

because I didn't realize then that this
would be a time worth telling

because youth is nearly the same thing
as being restless

because we spoke before we listened
correction: we shouted instead of listening

because we could feel the quicksand
at our feet

because childhood ends mid-sentence

because the black-wire tables cast in starlight
spoke to us of freedom

because desperation was our language
ancient as DNA

# WHAT WE'RE LOOKING FOR

The river dries up, and we discover
everything we have ever lost in it.
Hats that fell off when we leaned too far.
Glasses the water must have used

to magnify itself where the blind
creatures scuttle. We find the silly love
letters crumpled up, bleeding between words.
We were naïve, believing we were the falls.

A boat preserved in a bottle, tan sails
drawn for the trip ahead, forever
sailing toward the tight, brown cork
that keeps its journey eternally young.

Then we find what we're looking for,
leather bound bags of bones.
And we drag them back though they scream
*it is time, it is time.* We will not let go.

# NOT SIMPLY THE DARK

I turn on the light to bury the terror.
Soon, I am taken again by a dream:
a beautiful woman bathes in a chalice
singing poetry about money and love.
It has nothing to do with why
my light is on, or how I live as though
I will never die. Or how I worry
that happiness will never be enough.
I wake again and the light is still on.
I cannot bring myself to turn it off,
despite the dreams, and this is not
simply a fear of the dark. What I bury
in the dark will one day be unearthed.
I know why the light is there. I know
what I am trying to do.

# MENDING

I plunge my hands
into the dirt, and
like the earthworms
I have been rent
in two: one side crying,
head in my hands,
one side so distant
from myself
I look on and haunt.
Any loss makes home
retreat into the far,
far away, and where else
can I plant home
but with the sprouting
red rose bushes in this
good dirt where my dog,
Sprocket, would love
to dig if she were still
here, not stuck
in my mind's theater
with her eyes ghosting
back in a grey
vet's office. But she's not
only there, she's also
an after-image of white hair
running until the panting
catches in her throat,
and leaping at the ground
to dig up more dirt,
and telling everyone
with her nub of a tail
how happy she was
whenever I came home.
Oh if I had wishes
I would use these hands

to pull us back
from whatever unknowing
of each other we are
destined to enact.
And where is home
but in the fertile hills
of each other's imaginations,
so when I lose a friend,
even or especially a dog,
I might ask—*who am I?*
Again seventeen pondering
the too-big questions
in a green fleece jacket
and fedora under
the broad, deciduous leaves
of Manito Park, when
neither my pants nor
my ability to philosophize
fit my body or my heart.
I'm always
growing into them
and growing out of them
as time forces us out
of each brief heaven.
I pull my hands
from the wet
dirt, wiping them
on my jeans first,
then accidentally
onto my face as
I brush back my hair,
blessed now by
one stain that washes
off, and another
that remains.

# AT THE AUTO SHOP

If he is an old car
he could use a tune-up,
but he still runs.
He says he even knows
how to run on empty.

Not on empty,
on emptiness.

Our scientists disagree.
They can't issue patents
for something with no value.

That's just it.
It isn't no value,
it's "no" value.
Value found
that is the no of the value.
An entirely human thing.

Nothing human interests them,
old car;
there are new cars on the road.
*Move aside*, they say.
*Move aside.*

If he says *no*
they might not understand
it wasn't the same no
as the nothing no.

Outside we can find
a billion reasons to live,

but there aren't a billion things.
How can that be?

They aren't interested in that.
Give them something they can see.

But they can't see a thing.

He can run on the emptiness,
the nothingness, the no.

# THE TIN MAN

The rusty old tin man
waited years uncounted
and saw untold horrid
things. He is lucky to
have been rescued at all.
Not even he knows if
he can die. Or would have,
with his pale sentience
rusting to a standstill
as centuries whirled by
and decades gathered like
particles of dust at
his feet.

       As soon as they
oiled up his joints he danced
a jig. Sang a song. He'd
forgiven the world for
everything. That's how you
can tell it isn't real life.

# ORPHEUS LEARNS THE WOLF'S SONG

I had to break
my lyre, turn

wood to smoke
in the evanescent
forest above hell

as the faces
of Cerberus circled,

waiting for me
to sleep. I had to
sacrifice my gift,

to say goodbye
to the voice

that seduced death.
I had to burn
the path back.

I had to learn that
music disappears

as faces do. It hovers
for a moment
and is gone.

I knew then
why the beasts circled,

that they fear
fire, recognizing
the underworld as  I do.

And I knew then
why the stars go out.

And I knew then
why the night
is dark, and why

when the sun
dies the moon

will sing red,
red,
red.

# JELLYFISH ODE

O sea pillow
with murder for feet.
Do you mean
to sting
or only to drift
lazily on, carrying
as little
ill will
as the current,
happy or morose,
we cannot tell,
but certainly
without choice,
soft-headed torturer
of the underwater
rainforest. Jellyfish—
opposite of a
succulent, but still
cactus of the sea,
body of a half-sealed
ziploc bag
flushed down the
grime filled gutter,
inexplicably filled
with life
instead of a sandwich,
who needs
no brain, no face
to smile or cry,

no discernable
career goals or
student debt. Even so,
it's difficult
to imagine
your way
is better, you
who need
no thought, no
emotion but the
waves moving over
and through you.
I must admit
I too grabbed
the ocean
and stuffed myself
with it
hundreds of millions
of years ago,
sewing my skin
closed in
that far gone
era when you
had already
long reigned as
king of the
world, O master
of change
so slow
it may not

be happening
at all, change
so slow it
baffles us
who have eyes
to see when
you do not.
I tell you that we
are sacks of skin
and ambition.
We mean it when
we promise this
union, or that
pyramid, or our
footprint in
the stars will
last forever.
Yet it is you
who have been
chosen to stitch
the eons together
with a patience
that we who have
brains to
understand,
who are tasked
with discovering
the significance
of every ordinary
day, will never
comprehend.

# ODE TO STATIC

Fireflies      swarm      behind      electric

glass

as we sit forgetting how

to speak

our words      like ten thousand wings

covered in      molasses

struggling to

break free from a

black amber screen

igniting

for brief moments

sometimes

even

shining

through.

# THE ORIGIN OF BLIZZARDS

colors were all the rage rage rage

he dreamed sterile mechanisms
        black and white
                yes and no life and death

in a place where everyone had wings
        but no one could see them

no one had sprouted
        the flight he dreamed
                unsatisfied with human weight

why couldn't I have been born a bird
        he pleaded to the sky
                an egret or a skylark it wouldn't matter

he dreamed of flight
        cold and clear until
                it was all he could see

his god was the blank-faced
        god of december
                who sits upon a hallowed throne of snow

who judges the year by its end

                who judges wrong and right true and false

beginning
    where everything is at an end
        he who wished for wings prayed

the prayer of freezing things
                frost-weighted words
    a scratched-out calendar a fossilized jawbone

it took years

he built his wings
    one cold revelation at a time
        speck of snow by speck of snow

falling from the sky in years
    of december
        while no one bothered to look

            the tinker mad in his maze

    pain twists us into strange shapes

            pain created him in its image
        a person of cruel and clear and sudden
white wings

    meaning absence
    meaning contrast
    the hue of breath in the cold

he had his own answer
            heading to the cliff
                        courage is hard work and intellect

and a pain no one can understand
            look I'm flying

                        don't look

                  his wings are just snow
                  they can only bring the sky down
                  blanket the world in mourning

                        don't look at the ground
                        the impact getting closer
                        truth too far from the sun

                  he can see you
                  the blizzard cuts your heads off from him
                  you bump into each other and weep

                              it is all because of me
                        why did I write this person
                  to the edge of a cliff

                  to the throne of december
            who is the cruel king of the end of the world

                        who believes everything is an end
                        who believes everything must die

who presides over the season
                              where we must hold each other most close

I put us on the precipice
        with the wings of snow
              I bring the sky down

                                        no I write us back to the beginning
                              I write a storm backing away from the cliff
                    I write pain does not twist us

                        I write him spitting in december's face
              the hue of snow not illuminating the sky
        while wings the color of regret

do not bring down a sheet of absence
                            feathers suffocating the breath of sanity
I write him forgiving himself

        but I know I've lied        he's back at the precipice begging me to jump

colors are all the rage rage rage
                I write us back to the beginning
        I say he was the smartest kid in his class

              I say everyone liked him
I tell you this but he dreams life a sterile mechanism
        a hurt mask destroying a whole world

I say everything will be okay

we'll run away from this poem
but december can last years

I've seen years no one smiles
at all
                    and my friends walk to the cliff

        and I do not know how to stop them
                    I write a different story I need to know it's true
                            I recognize my lying face

                        writing at a mirror

                            why couldn't you have been born a bird
                        an egret or a skylark
            it wouldn't matter

                    your wings would have held up
        a starlit sea of eyes
            but the wings I gave you can only bring the sky down

                    I write us to the cliff
        I want to save us
                    I write a quiet december

stupid brain
stupid story stupid writer
why do you think you can write away quiet suicide without

        screaming

december who is summer
december who does not answer dismal prayers
december who is not a god of loneliness

colors were all the rage rage rage
and though he dreamed mechanisms of loss
as though loss were life

as though rage were something
to hold close stupid brain
that's what you do isn't it

colors were all the rage rage rage
I can learn nothing from death
rage and we don't know why

stupid story brain
rushing water turned hard by height
won't solve any of your problems

is this how god writes our stories
hiding behind a hallowed paper throne
shattered by what has been done

a labyrinth of absence
architect caught escaping
his own creation

rage rage rage and there must be something wrong
when our wings bring the sky down

so much contrast adding up to blankness in my heart
damn story heart

stupid story brain

saying coward
                              saying why
                                                  I write him stronger
                                                        I write him too smart

                         I write him too beautiful
              I write him in love
                                   damned writer heart

                                             I write it is not your fault
                                             I write you are not a burden

rage and the white-out blocking me from the truth

rage and the poor story pacing the cliff

rage and why do the people I love want to die

                                             he is at the cliff begging
I am always there with him

he is at the cliff begging

searching up at me face twisted with what
                              with why

      one foot over the edge
one foot stepping back

62

# GOD SPEAKS AS A PARKING ATTENDANT

I love my creations.
How their faces purse up violet to speak at me,
begging forgiveness. I love
how they believe they are lying
when they promise me nothing is their fault.
I love the simple, upright machine
counting down time, bestowing on my glorious
images the gift of temporality.
A vehicle must be in one place, then another.
A vehicle must move through the void.
I gifted them this void,
how it haunts, cradling them
like an abscessed tooth,
every truth they stuff themselves with rotting away
and all they want is to see me.
I love how none of them thanks me
for the limits I grew into their sight.
They see a black jacket, a printed sheet of numbers.
Not one looks into these eyes.
Not one discovers what happens to those
who catch sight of this mundane magnanimity.
I love the strong arm beneath a suit coat,
how I grew those muscles and tendons,
those little weak hairs that could not even
blink one sun out of existence,
the billions of years I spent
sculpting this vice that clasps my shoulder
saying, *mercy, or else, do I know who he is,*
*mercy,* the breath moves through the mouth
of this image, this glorious, divine image
who will not even recognize mercy

when it comes.

# THREE

# LULLABY

Lullaby, I've done you wrong.
There were nights I'd staple

my eyelids open to arrive
deliriously into day—

with no use for the honeysuckle
song of sleep, or bad dreams

banging banjos against gravestones.
Who rests here? Surely not me.

Not peacefully relented
like the cicada Rip Van Winkling

from stern Morpheus'
century-long thrall to find

I'd missed the brood, the flight,
the fireworked frenzy of each

new moment. There were nights
I honestly thought I could stop

life from passing me by, that I could
untether the sun's horses

from their lodestone shackles and thus stall
that iron chariot from racing through the sky.

Lullaby, I am not wise,
but I will gladly go

into your dark basement.
I will apologize. I will crawl

the ten thousand miles of the kingdom
of sleep to rattle my sand scorched palm

thricely against your melodic door.
If you will let me rest,

if you will declare armistice
over the empire of my body,

if you will lull me through the soft
plummet of sound into the unknowable,

unchartable arms of slumber.

# I MAKE THE BED

The sheet falls back to the bed, damp from one of those sweat-through
      nightmare nights, when I throw off
    blankets and sheets, and the sweat
        and dead skin cells cling to the fabric,
          part of the body even if they are not to be exalted.
I can't know what my own body feels like
dreaming against that white linen. I wonder.
        and I wonder how it is we dream,
        how the moment I realize I am flying
            I plummet, lead-winged.
Then there's these tiny brown arm-hairs, curling,
barely even part of me before they fall off,
unintelligibly stuck on the sheets even through
the washer's hot water whirl, where perishes
            a thin microbe menagerie.
          This too is life. It has nucleus,
          cell membrane, cilia, and the mitochondria,
          hammer and sickle of the cell.
            This too is life in a world separate
            but in the same place
            I struggle to call my home.
I really do like it here. Only it's not so simple
as putting my own sheets on the bed,
waiting until enough of me falls off
that when I push my broom gliding across the floor I say,
      *Where did all of this come from?*
          It is only me here, me and the sheets
          I stretch flat over the bed.
            I really do like living. I like
            waking up in the morning and falling

back to sleep in those thread-counts
that come more undone each time
I whirl them through their
scalding water heaven.
Soon, the bedding will grow holes,
and I could throw it over my head
and be again a child, floating through the house
saying *booooooooooooo* giving my mother
a true frightening before tossing off the costume
saying, *look it's only me.*
It's still only me. I still want to be alive.
I still kick off blankets, scared, awakening
enshrouded by the awareness that death will happen to me,
and then what will my microbes do,
my skin cells, my hair, and me
the ghost, will there even be a thing to sweep up—
what will happen to my breath that fogs
the brittle window of Autumn, my finger
making a print in condensation.
I want to be composed when the moment comes.
I want to be ready to be a ghost or a nothing.
Being loved, being remembered, liking living
cannot prepare me for the profession
of a headstone—the fresh morning's dew
feeding red lichen in each letter of my name.

After the night's turbulent sleep I make the bed.
First the sheets, then the blankets, then the pillows.
And when the time comes I part the curtains
and let in the astonishing day.

# THE CROWN LEAVES SCATTER

*For Ted Potter*

Wandering in a pine grove
I find an obsolete, yellow refrigerator,
the kind that even unplugged can hold

a cold, belligerent truth.
A one-way door, I try prying it open
to know what silent deep it keeps hidden,

and the handle comes off in my grip.
Inside the rusted metal
ancient bees nest dry as paper

guarding the stilled young
they had hoped
to keep precious to the wild

astonishment of being. The nest falls
to the ground like crushed and dried
blossoms. It joins the green tinsel

of the forest floor, soon to be simplified by
fungus and the stomachs of worms, dreams
forever fled delivering

good news about the state of mystery.
If only I could make myself porous
to the worms' words, I would bend my neck

to the silent, deep dirt, listen for what
they do with our dreams forever fled.
Perhaps I'd hear something

of Tom Bell, my first ancestor to live
in this pine grove now called Spangle.
Tom Bell whose poem I am to read

at a family gathering in a house bordering
this green shroud of festered wonder.
A poem that crawled in almost illegible lines

across his diary's open face
after his wife's death: on the previous
page a list of twenty-one names

captioned, "Memorial cards sent
to friends." A poem like the day
by night overshadowed

by the heavy cowl of those names.
The weathered seeds listening to me read beg,
it's a good poem, isn't it, for how old it is?

Tom, I see you on your knees
turning to these words, these ink scrawls
like roses torn and faded.

I'd like to think we'd be friends
if we had been born in the same century.
You are remembered as a good man,

and that is nearly all I know.
Though age has been callous to rhyme,
I pick through these lines,

parse through the thicket
of our unknowing, into the truth of you,
writing for an answer because there is not one.

The ink wet and smudging, it comes out,
"Crown leaves scatter," "Beauty fades
and roses perish." I reach my fingers

to the door. One hundred years enter
the silent deep. The handle comes off
in my grip. It comes out,

"Day by night overshadowed."
"Roses torn and faded." I want to know you
and all I have are these words

wet with an absence you found illegible.
Bees crawl inside each and every syllable
and dry thin as paper. I wonder

what is hiding inside but the state
of mystery is a palace too lavish
of "Silent deep." I reach my hand

to the door. I hear your pen
scratch against the paper. Cousins
who are your crown leaves scattered

ask if it was a good poem.
The door to the silent deep
falls into my hands. Today it is a leaf

of paper. If I'm gentle enough
I can feel bees buzzing beneath,
soft as a buried pulse.

# I WILL BUY AN ORCHID AND PUT IT ON THE TABLE WHERE TOGETHER WE WILL GROW

I unpack the boxes, stare
down the ceiling, mark the day.
There are no memories here,

no whispers from love letters
wall-papered over, unreaped.
I unpack the boxes. Stairs

creak down to a door, my door.
So, you could say I feel free.
There are no memories. Here,

I could plant a life, could shear
my skull of gone stale ghosts. Me,
I unpack. The boxes stare,

letting go leaves like a dare.
Can I let myself let go
there? Are no memories here

to have and to hold, to part
or break deciduous days?
I unpack. The boxes stare.
There are no memories here.

# SONNET FOR MICA, WASHINGTON

Up on a dream where I remember boyhood,
Beyond the thorn-thick bramble children here
Each discover their way through, over wire
Barbed before my birth but still sharp enough,

Past the branches snapping back, the scratches,
Cuts and the itch of already healing,
Where crabgrass overlooks a gold wheat field
Off the Marietta hill waits a bench:

Just a couple of boards clumsy with nails,
A violet evening vision of first love's sails,
A dream-rich kingdom of lips' innocence
I pictured before I knew what kisses meant

While beyond this thorn-thick bramble body
My heart, always eager, leapt without me.

# TULIPS

When I say—*For the third time*
*he entered the grain elevator,*
*and now he found it*
*completely filled with tulips—*

I do not simply mean
the grain had been replaced
due to a hero's trial.
The tulips are useless.
He wished
for a full elevator
but he didn't specify with grain.
Then he walks around town
giving the tulips to children,
putting them to the best use he can.

## YO-YO / SCARECROW / ROCKFORD FAIR / ERGO SUM

I am the yo-yo / I am *in* the yo-yo / a carnival's whirl / at the Rockford Fair / hard to tell where I end in the spinning / where the wind begins / in my ears / in the stories drifting up from neon /

the giggle behind me wrapped in an autumn scarf / I spent my last dollars on bingo here decades ago / dreaming questions of who will love me / how soon / why not yet / and if I could

go back with the wind would I tell him not to worry / in the waiting hay / the braying animals in their barn / or would I remain silent / why spoil the surprise / over thirty years old and hardly

growing rampant / little lovely weed / trying to prove himself a flower / I notice the grey trailers hidden behind the rides, haphazard homes / knowing this is daily life / permits and pieces of

paper pushed across desks / overnight kingdom of mystery / only real people working / this life not always what we make of it / not only what it makes of us / I ask we may smile on the auburn

fall day we are brought to harvest / I dreamed for so many years of having someone by my side, bringing them here, saying this is where I ran free / looking out from the height of the Ferris

wheel / silly scarecrow at the top of the world / what's he got to prove / scarecrow racing the dizzy highway / ninety miles per hour / it's all a field of wheat somehow, huh / only with gelled

78

hair / I have a house of mirrors with your name on it / see your face in every face / your long hollow eyes / lost in faraway constellations / on the good nights, back against the cool

grass finding nowhere's middle / recognizing yourself in every filthy thing / struggling to be redeemed / as a blackbird glints across the fresh-faced moon / and the wind gives back my

secrets / chickens and rabbits waiting in their cages / ribbons that don't mean a thing to them / the chill setting in / I want to feel it all / in the center of this whirling moment / I am buying a

magic trick / picturing myself with a cape / I am painting a face onto a zucchini / his eyes peering out in a smile / where is my blue ribbon / I could never throw him away / he is shriveling up / he

is barely a memory / I am saying I won this prize for you / will you take it / will you remember me when I am gone / little scarecrow, here is a wall of balloons and the fine dart blade of longing /

the whir, pop, clamor, and bang / here is a brain / think me up a good question / think me up a good song / you've won it all / congratulations congratulations / a plush rabbit filled with

sawdust / who can only say / I love / I am love / I am love therefore I am.

79

# SONNET IN THE FORM OF A BUBBLE BATH

*For Emerald*

For you, I would overflow with warmth,
Becoming the claw-foot bathtub in my old
Apartment, giggling as lavender bubbles
Drip down my ceramic sides. For you

I would become antique, gazing out
The window as leaves change color
On a green hill. I would eat by oil lamp
In cold porcelain, patient waiting.

One day you will enter through an old oak door
Without needing to knock. In the twilight
Of a fogged breath afternoon you will sip
From a burgundy glass, turning my faucet

With your toe: my teeth, lavender bubbles
As the sun sets, swallowing every curve of you.

# THE KITE

When he is asked of his relationship
with the wind, the kite answers—

*She pushes,*
*I push back.*
*She always wins,*
*but I get to fly.*

# THE CLOUD SPEAKS

When I whisper, the little dots shiver,
point at their statues and say
*Look. They are crying, like us.*

Better to be a cloud than to hurt so much,
to cry into my face pleading mercy.
They shall have their mercy
when the oceans turn to dust.

These little dots shake when I cleave
the sky in two with my jagged jawline.
Its flash illuminating the hair's-breadth
chasm between worship and terror:
my voice too loud to speak over.
Some still love beneath,
their drenched faces implicating me
in the tongue-tangled history of kissing.

But I also invented the rust on the nail.
My proudest attribute:
that I will wear everything away,
even those testaments to forever
the little dots wrap around each other's fingers.

Silver, gold, titanium, diamond—
it does not matter.

I know something of this forever
the little dots do not.

How much of their ash I have washed from hillsides,
sending myself down in great billowing wallows
to lift the grey dust of grief as it sifts
between their fingers, carrying it downstream
where it may finally rest.

I know it is best they cannot hold on
to what has passed, though they disagree

pointing at the red streaks I paint
beneath the eyelids of their finally honest
hollow artworks. Their saints, their Marys,
their lady of liberty, as they say,
*Please, promise me we do not cry like that.*

Better to dissipate at the slightest touch
of heat than wear such unrelenting weather.

I mimic flames in the river's pale lisp,
screaming *stay back* as the saddest little dots
hurl themselves into my white,
clamoring teeth pleading mercy.

If only their corrosion were as simple as rust,
iron baking in the rain: changing,
if not for better, at least by law.

At times I condense between
these little dots and their bathroom mirrors,
suggesting they treat themselves with mercy.

After all, I am also in them,

coming out of their breath in those bedrooms
where they spend the heaven of their flesh.
I weigh the space between those walls
heavy as the sky with my million little eyes,
preparing, as always, to fall.

Chilled in the morning's exhale
I settle on the skin of a nail she used
to carve their initials in a tree's browning bark,
framing their future in a heart
or an arrow pointing down.

There on the nail, too small to be seen,
I grow an orchard of crimson and orange:
the blossoming for which steel secretly yearns.

Always too quiet or loud to be heard
I scream, and I scream, and I scream.

I will cleanse this world of everything.

# CATCHING THE RAIN

Sadness, you were my answer as I stood
blue in the field, raindrops: little clear
dots wrapping me in the atmosphere.

I thought you were beautiful, Sadness. I said
*Someone take a picture of this*. I looked
to the clouds, a thick gray sermon

letting fall locusts of rain. I stuck out
my tongue to tickle as a droplet came down
point first, ending in an imperceptible splash.

Sadness, I made a god of you, if a god is what
we worship, and if to worship is to fall to your knees.
I thought you were making me beautiful. Someone

take a picture of this. I felt the drop impact
and disappear on my taste buds. I tasted
the dirt it absorbed from the air. I wanted

to be Happiness, but Sadness I thought
I could use you or get used to you, that the only
useful color was blue. I said *I feel this*.

I saw my face reflected in water
and in what raindrops do.

# A COMFORTABLE HOME

It's where the cat knows
enough of the alphabet
to walk across the laptop
imagining itself a famous novelist.
I want to tell the cat
it's not the novelist's job
to be famous, only to write.
In a comfortable home no one
has to worry about fame or riches.
Instead, they are satisfied
with pulling warm bread
out of an old oven,
letting it rise softer than a pillow,
filling every brick of the house
with its scent. A crackling fire
to ward off the cold.
The only reason to go outside
is to look at the moon, wave hello
to the man camped there hoarding
detachment. Tell him
he is doing a good job.
We came to the Earth to have
feelings. If anyone says *no more*
*moon poems for you,* you are allowed
to tell them they are wrong.
The monster under the bed
is reading a book. Invite him
into the lamp's light.
Read it word by word.

My immense gratitude to the editors of the following publications for sharing my work with their readers and giving it life:

*The Pacific Northwest Inlander*: "In the Afterworld I Encounter All the Things I've Lost," "The Cloud Speaks"; *Art Chowder*: "The Elves and the Shoemaker at Mica Cemetery"; *Spokane/Coeur d'Alene Living*: "Innocence"; *The Spokesman Review*: "So You Want Me to Fall in Love With You," "Sonnet for Mica, Washington"; *Drunk in a Midnight Choir*: "Dandelions"; *Railtown Almanac*: "I Spent My Summer Nights on the Patio of Old Empyrean"; *Terrain.org*: "Children Discover an Electric Fence and the Direction of Time"

"On the Size of Wings," I wrote for a limited-run book published by Spark Central called *Starstruck*.

"Mending," I wrote for a collaborative show at Coeur d'Alene's Emerge, inspired by a painting of the same name by Gracey Laursen. The show was called *Ekphrastic Fantastic*.


My first and endless thanks to my parents for believing in me and nurturing my creativity, for reading me books and writing out my stories and poems before I could write them myself.

Kurt Olson, Danielle Estelle Ramsay, Zack Graham, Michael Schomburg, Lauren Gilmore, Isaac Grambo, Stephen Meads, Chris Leja, Taylor Rose, Ryler Dustin, Dennis Held, Laura Read, Kathryn Smith, Brooke Matson, Jonathan Potter, Thom Caraway; thank you for writing with me, for your steadfast feedback and support, and for sharing countless stages with these poems. Out of all the possible books I could have made from these poems, thank you for helping me to find the best one.

Thank you to Mrs. Bernhard, my second-grade teacher, for being the first person outside of my family to call me a poet.

And finally, the entirety of my love and gratitude to Emerald.

MARK L. ANDERSON lives and writes in Spokane, Washington. He co-founded the popular Broken Mic spoken word poetry series and has traveled the United States performing at open mics, poetry slams, taverns, coffee shops, and libraries. From 2017 to 2019, he served as Spokane's poet laureate.

Made in USA - Kendallville, IN
58561_9780983151364
11 11 2026 1206